Skills Builders

SB

Lever Edge Primary Academy

YEAR 1

ENGLISH

Sarah Turner

Acknowledgements

Every effort has been made to trace all copyright holders, but if any have been inadvertently overlooked, the Publishers will be pleased to make the necessary arrangements at the first opportunity.

Although every effort has been made to ensure that website addresses are correct at time of going to press, Rising Stars cannot be held responsible for the content of any website mentioned in this book. It is sometimes possible to find a relocated web page by typing in the address of the home page for a website in the URL window of your browser.

Hachette UK's policy is to use papers that are natural, renewable and recyclable products and made from wood grown in sustainable forests. The logging and manufacturing processes are expected to conform to the environmental regulations of the country of origin.

ISBN: 978-1-78339-689-4

Text, design and layout © 2015 Rising Stars UK Ltd

First published in 2015 by Rising Stars UK Ltd

Reprinted March 2016

Rising Stars UK Ltd,
An Hachette UK Company
Carmelite House
50 Victoria Embankment
London EC4Y 0DZ
www.risingstars-uk.com

All facts are correct at time of going to press.

Author: Sarah Turner
Educational Consultant: Madeleine Barnes
Publisher: Laura White
Illustrator: Emily Skinner
Logo design: Amparo Barrera, Kneath Associates Ltd
Design: Julie Martin
Typesetting: Words & Pictures, London
Cover design: Amparo Barrera, Kneath Associates Ltd
Project Manager: Emily Wilson
Copy Editor: Sparks Publishing Services, Ltd
Proofreader: Gemma Batty
Software development: Alex Morris

British Library Cataloguing-in-Publication Data

A CIP record for this book is available from the British Library.

Printed by Newnorth Ltd, Kempston, Bedford

Contents

1 Ordering letters of the alphabet

There are 26 letters of the alphabet.

They go in a special order.

a b c d e f g h i j k l m n o p q r s t u v w x y z

Activity 1

Can you put the letters in the correct order?

h o p y u q w a d g x k
e t b f c i l m r j
n s v z

Activity 2

Can you work out which letters are missing?

a	b		d		f	g		i		k	l
n	o		q	r			u		w		y

Investigate!

Can you find any places in the classroom where some of the letters of the alphabet are in order?

2 Lower case and capital letters

We can write our letters in two different ways.

lower case letter   capital letter

a   A

b   B

Activity 1

Can you write the lower case letter next to the correct capital letter?

D   **H**   **I**   **L**   **N**

n   i   h   d   l

Activity 2

Can you complete the pairs of lower case and capital letters?

a = A

a) _____ = D   b) k = _____   c) _____ = G

d) _____ = V   e) p = _____   f) _____ = Z

g) _____ = Q   h) e = _____   i) _____ = R

Investigate!

Can you find capital letters in your classroom? Draw pictures of the different places you find them.

5

3 ff and ll

When we want to write the *f* sound we usually use ff after a short vowel sound.

cliff   fluff

Activity 1

Can you add **ff** to each of these words? What are the words? Can you find the odd one out?

a) sti _____   **b)** cu _____   **c)** stu _____   **d)** i _____

e) o _____   **f)** scu _____   **g)** sta _____   **h)** gru _____

When we want to write the *l* sound we use ll after a short vowel sound.

bell   till

Activity 2

Can you add **ll** to each of these words? What are the words?

a) fi _____   **b)** do _____   **c)** bi _____   **d)** sme _____

e) gu _____   **f)** se _____   **g)** te _____   **h)** fe _____

4 ck and nk

When we want to write the *k* sound we use ck after a short vowel sound.

sock   **rock**

Activity 1

Can you add **ck** to each of these words? What are the words?

a) pi _____   **b)** bla _____   **c)** blo _____   **d)** ne _____

e) du _____   **f)** qui _____   **g)** thi _____   **h)** clo _____

Some words end with the sound *nk* – spelt nk. This can be a bit tricky to hear and say.

sink   **wink**

Activity 2

Can you add **nk** to each of these words? What are the words?

a) ba _____   **b)** pi _____   **c)** thi _____   **d)** i _____

e) ta _____   **f)** ri _____   **g)** ho _____   **h)** su _____

5 tch and v

The *ch* sound is usually spelt with a silent *t* – tch – after a short vowel sound.

catch   fetch   itch

Activity 1

Can you add **tch** to each of these words? What are the words?

a) ma _____   **b)** i _____   **c)** ca _____   **d)** fe _____

e) hu _____   **f)** ki _____ en   **g)** sti _____   **h)** ha _____

If a word sounds like it ends with a *v* then it usually has an *e* after it.

love   dove

Activity 2

Can you add **ve** to each of these words? What are the words?

a) abo _____   **b)** glo _____   **c)** ha _____   **d)** li _____

e) gi _____   **f)** ali _____   **g)** ca _____   **h)** di _____

6 ss and zz

When we want to write the *s* sound we usually use **ss** after a short vowel sound.

glass   chess

Activity 1

Can you add **ss** to each of these words? What are the words? Can you find the odd ones out?

a) dre _____   **b)** me _____   **c)** bu _____   **d)** hi _____

e) ki _____   **f)** cla _____   **g)** ye _____   **f)** bo _____

When we want to write the *z* sound we use **zz** after a short vowel sound.

buzz   fizz

Activity 2

Can you add **zz** to each of these words? What are the words?

a) ja _____   **b)** fu _____   **c)** bu _____

Investigate!

Can you write a sentence with one of these words in?

buzz   fizz   jazz   fuzz

7 Singular and plural

One of something is called singular.

More than one is called plural.

For most words, we add s to make it plural.

singular   plural
one dog   ⟶   two dogs
one apple ⟶   lots of apples

Activity 1

Can you make a list of the matching singular and plural words?

one ball ⟶ two balls

one banana   one ball   one bird   one cup

two birds   two cups   two bananas   two balls

Activity 2

Can you change these singular words to a plural?

a) flower   b) hat   c) car   d) girl

e) egg   f) bag   g) rock   h) pencil

If a word ends in *s, ss, sh, ch, tch, x* or *z*, we add es to make it plural.

singular   plural

one dress ⟶ **two** dresses

one peach ⟶ **lots of** peaches

Activity 3

Can you change these words to plural? Don't forget the rule!

a) lunch   **b)** dish   **c)** waltz   **d)** bus

e) wish   **f)** glass   **g)** fix   **h)** stitch

Activity 4

Can you work out the correct spelling of the plural words below?

a) fish = fishs or fishes?

b) fox = foxs or foxes?

c) watch = watchs or watches?

d) church = churchs or churches?

Investigate!

How many words can you find in your reading books where you add **s** to make it plural?

How many words can you find in your reading books where you add **es** to make it plural?

8 Naming objects and things

All objects, living things and places have a name.
We call the name of something a naming word (noun).

object	living thing	place
table	bird	beach

Activity 1

Can you draw five objects from around the room and name them?

desk

Activity 2

Can you find the naming words (nouns) in each of the sentences below? There might be more than one in each sentence!

a) The elephant was plodding slowly.

b) The girl likes to play board games.

c) The lion was resting in the tall grass after eating the meat.

Investigate!

How many naming words (nouns) can you think of around your school?

9 Action words

All sentences have *doing* or *being* words in them. We call these words action words (verbs).

The footballer kicks the ball.

Activity 1

Which action word below finishes each of the sentences?

played   jumped   is   am   are

a) The girl _____ over the wall.

b) The boys _____ chess together.

c) She _____ a teacher.

d) I _____ a child.

e) They _____ friends.

Activity 2

Write the action word (verb) for each of the pictures.

a)   b)   c)   d)

10 What is a sentence?

A sentence is a group of words that tell the reader something.

A sentence has a subject (noun) and an action word (verb).

A sentence starts with a capital letter and ends with a full stop.

The cat sat down.

Activity 1

Which are sentences? Can you write them down?

The cow ate some grass.

The girl went to the

The children went to the cinema to watch a film.

My mum is

Activity 2

These sentences are jumbled up. Can you put them in the correct order?

a) the sky. The sun shining in was

b) at the had park. Jack and I lunch

Activity 3

Can you finish off these sentences so that they make sense? Remember to use a full stop at the end.

a) Jack liked to bake _____

b) The dinosaur had a _____

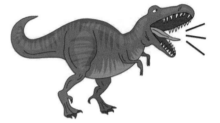

c) The princess wanted to _____

d) This car can _____

11 Adding the suffixes ing and ed

We add **ing** to action words (verbs) to say something is happening now – it is in the present.

We eat the cake. ⟶ **We are eating the cake.**

Activity 1

Can you write down the matching pairs?

pull – **pulling**

go   meet   do

doing   going   meeting

Activity 2

Can you change the action word by adding **ing**?

a) The dog **follows** the cat.

The dog is _____ the cat.

b) The boy **kicks** the ball.

The boy is _____ the ball.

We add ed to action words (verbs) to say that something has happened – is it in the past.

We climb **the ladder.** ⟶ **We** climbed **the ladder.**

Activity 3

Can you write down the matching pairs?

park – parked

look   help   paint   walk

helped   walked   looked   painted

Activity 4

Can you change these sentences so they are happening in the past?

a) Tomorrow I will work in a cake shop.

Yesterday I _____ in a cake shop.

b) Today I will play with my friends.

Yesterday I _____ with my friends.

12 Adding the suffix er

We add **er** to an action word (verb) to change it to a naming word (noun).

help ⟶ helper

Activity 1

Can you match the present and past action words to the naming words?

climbing — climbed — climber

hunting   buzzing   jumping   buzzed

buzzer   jumped   hunted

jumper   hunter

Activity 2

Can you write three sentences using any of the words above?

Investigate!

Can you find some other action words that end in **ing** or **ed**?
Can you change these action words to naming words?

13 Adding the prefix un

When we add the letters **un** to a word we make an opposite word.

happy ⟶ **unhappy**

Activity 1

Can you change these words to the opposite meaning by adding **un**?

a) kind **b)** helpful **c)** lucky

d) well **e)** load **f)** lock

Activity 2

Can you write three sentences that each use one of the new **un** words you have created? Here are some examples to help you.

My dog is unwell.

My dad unlocked the car.

We had to unload the boxes from the truck.

Investigate!

How many words can you think of that begin with the letters **un**?

14 Adding er and est

We add er or est to a describing word (adjective) to compare it to another object.

The boy was quick.
The girl was quicker.
The dog was the quickest.

Activity 1

Can you match the root words with their er and est words?

slow – slower – slowest

bright   great   full   deep

greater   deeper   brighter   fuller

deepest   fullest   greatest   brightest

Activity 2

Can you finish these sentences using er and est words.

a) The wind was cold.

The water was _____ .

The ice was the _____ .

b) The tree was high.

The hill was _____ .

The mountain was the _____ .

15 Using and as a joining word

We can join two short sentences together using **and**.

Max went home. He had tea.
Max went home and he had tea.

Activity 1

Can you join these sentences together using the word **and** so that they make sense?

Jake had his supper.
I love eating chocolate.
It is a beautiful day.

and

The sun is shining.
He had a hot chocolate.
I enjoy eating ice-cream.

Activity 2

Can you finish these sentences so that they make sense?

a) Amir was walking down the road **and** _____ .

b) Sasha liked to dress up as a princess **and** _____ .

c) It was a hot day **and** _____ .

Investigate!

Can you join two sentences using the joining word **but**? What is the difference?

21

16 Capital letters

The first word of every sentence must start with a capital letter.

The rain made puddles on the ground.

Activity 1

Can you put a capital letter in the correct place in each sentence?

a) it was cold and dark in the forest.

b) the children made sandcastles on the beach.

c) how many sweets can we have each?

The name of a person or place also needs a capital letter.

The Queen lives in London.

Activity 2

Which pictures need a capital letter because they are the name of a place or person?

a) big ben   b) bag   c) jack   d) pencil   e) united kingdom

Activity 3

Can you write down the words in these sentences that should have a capital letter?

a) my brother's dog is called charlie.

b) jake and robert are going on holiday to spain.

c) what will you wear for the party?

d) ayesha is going to the cinema to watch cinderella.

> **The word I, when you are writing about yourself, is also always a capital letter.**
>
> **Kirsty and I like to go shopping.**

Activity 4

Can you find all of the mistakes in the sentence below? Write it again using capital letters.

lucy and i are going to a birthday party on friday.

Investigate!

How many different words can you list that need to have a capital letter to start them?

17 Full stops

We use a full stop (.) to tell the reader a sentence is finished and they should pause.

The monkey climbs in the trees.

Activity 1

The full stops are in the wrong places. Can you write the sentences correctly?

a) We had roast beef and potatoes. for our dinner

b) The teacher sang. a song with the children

c) After lunch we went. to play at the park

Activity 2

Can you write three sentences about this picture using capital letters and full stops in the correct places?

24

18 Question marks

A question is something you ask someone when you want to find something out.

When we ask a question we need to finish the sentence with ?

What time is it?

Activity 1

Can you write the sentences and add a question mark?

a) What are you having for lunch

b) Where are you going on your holiday

c) Why do we need to go to school

Activity 2

Can you write three questions about this picture?

19 Exclamation marks

Exclamation marks are used at the end of a sentence to show excitement, worry, surprise or anger.

The sentence often starts with How or What.

What a lovely day!   **How exciting!**

Activity 1

Can you write the sentences and add an exclamation mark?

a) What a fantastic drawing

b) How clever of you

c) What wonderful news

You can also use an exclamation mark after a single word to show you are surprised or in a hurry.

Help!   **Oops!**   **Ouch!**

Activity 2

Can you draw a picture of a face to show how you would feel if you said the following?

Uh-oh!   **Mmm!**   **Yes!**   **Oops!**

a)   b)   c)

20 Separating words with spaces

The spaces between each word in a sentence help us to read it.

Evalikestodressupasaprincess.
Eva likes to dress up as a princess.

Activity 1

Can you re-write these sentences leaving spaces between each word?

a) Tiaenjoys**playing**with**her**friends**at**nursery.

b) Acaterpillarchanges**into**a**beautiful**butterfly.

c) Inthe**morning**I**get**dressed**and**walk**to**school**.

d) Ihad**beans**on**toast**for**my**dinner**.

e) Shefound**a**big**crab**on**the**beach.

Investigate!

Can you use the words below to write some sentences of your own? Remember to leave spaces between the words!

book   read   school   dragon   knight   fire

castle   key   horse

21 Words ending in y

When a word ends with a long e sound it can be spelt with a y.

happy   party

Activity 1

Can you write the correct spelling to match the picture? They all end with a y.

a)

b _____

b)

l _____

c)

sp _____

d)

libr _____

Activity 2

Can you use these words to complete the sentences?

very   funny   family   party

a) The girl went to the _____ .

b) The clown was very _____ .

c) We are going on a _____ holiday.

22 ai, ay and a-e

There are different ways to spell the long *a* sound.

ai	ay	a-e
train	play	safe

Activity 1

Can you sort these words into **ai**, **ay** or **a-e** spellings?

day   made   rain   say   came   wait   way

same   paid   stay   take   afraid

Activity 2

Can you work out how to spell these words using **ai**, **ay** or **a-e**?

a)

wh _____

b)

sn _____

c)

br _____

d)

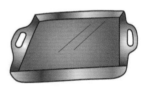

tr _____

23 oa, oe, o-e, and ow

There are different ways to spell the long *o* sound.

oa	oe	o-e	ow
b**oa**t	t**oe**	r**o**s**e**	arr**ow**

Activity 1

Can you sort these words into **oa**, **oe**, **o-e** or **ow** spellings?

oak   woe   those   foe   home   grow   goes

show   hole   hope   blow   woke

Activity 2

Can you work out how to spell these words using **oe**, **oa**, **ow** or **o-e**?

a)

b)

c)

d)

st _____

t _____

wind _____

b _____

Activity 3

Can you find the correct spelling to match the picture?

a)    boan   bone   bown

b)    goat   gowt   gote

c)    cowt   coat   cote

d)    phone   phown   phoen

Investigate!

How many long *o* sounds can you find around the classroom?

24 oi and oy

Here are two different ways to spell the same sound.

oi	oy
c**oi**n	j**oy**

Activity 1

Can you sort these words into **oi** and **oy** spellings?

oil   boy   join   buoy   coin   point   enjoy

soil   annoy   coil

Activity 2

Can you spell the words for these pictures? Will you use **oi** or **oy**?

a)

b)

c)

d)

b _____

cowb _____

f _____

t _____ s

25 ou and ow

Here are two different ways to spell the same sound.

ou	ow
mouse	cow

Activity 1

Can you sort these words into **ou** and **ow** spellings?

out   now   about   mouth   how · brown

around   down   sound   town

Activity 2

Can you unscramble the letters to find words to match the pictures?

a)

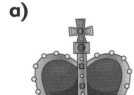

ow n cr

b)

ow n fr

c)

se ou h

d)

d ou cl

26 ee, ea, ie and i-e

There are different ways to spell the long e sound.

ee	ea	ie	e-e
tree	sea	chief	theme

Activity 1

Can you sort these words into **ee**, **ea**, **ie** or **e-e** spellings?

see   dream   thief   theme   these   seen   meet

week   meat   each   read

Activity 2

Can you unscramble the letters to find words to match the pictures?

a)

ie f l d

b)

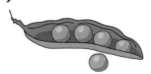

s ea p

c)

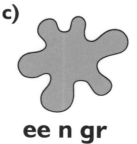

ee n gr

d)

ch ea b

34

Activity 3

Can you spell the words and use the correct long *e* sound to match the pictures?

a)   **b)**   **c)**   **d)**

str _____   sc _____   cook _____   sh _____

Investigate!

Can you find six more words in the grid with the long *e* sound? Make a list!

e	a	c	h	q	e	r	t	y	u
a	s	d	f	g	r	e	e	n	x
z	x	c	c	h	i	e	f	v	b
q	w	w	e	r	t	y	u	i	o
m	e	a	t	c	v	b	w	n	s
n	m	c	d	f	g	w	e	e	k
s	e	a	r	f	h	b	w	m	a
r	t	y	u	i	j	v	e	x	a
s	h	e	e	p	k	i	y	h	f
q	w	e	r	r	l	y	u	j	b

27 oo, u-e, ue and ew

There are different ways we can spell the long _u_ sound.

oo	u-e	ue	ew
sp**oo**n	t**u**b**e**	gl**ue**	scr**ew**

Activity 1

Can you unscramble the letters to find words to match the pictures?

a)

oo n m

b)

u-e n t

c)

b ue l

d)

r ew g

Activity 2

Can you sort these words into **oo**, **u-e, ue** or **ew** spellings?

food   few   true   pool   rescue   zoo   rule

drew   clue   soon   use

Activity 3

Can you choose the correct word for each of the questions and write a sentence?

new   blew   grew   flew   chew

a) What do you do with your food?

b) What did the wind do?

c) What did the bird do?

d) What is the opposite of old?

e) What did we do to stop being small?

Investigate!

Can you find seven more words in the grid with the long *u* sound? Make a list!

b	l	u	e	a	s	s	o	o	n
q	w	e	r	n	e	w	d	f	g
a	s	d	f	g	d	s	w	q	e
t	o	o	t	h	d	f	g	h	j
z	x	c	v	b	n	s	h	o	e
g	r	e	w	f	t	y	u	i	p
a	s	d	f	g	h	u	t	r	a
q	w	s	c	h	o	o	l	a	s
z	x	c	v	b	n	m	i	o	p
r	e	s	c	u	e	d	f	g	h

28 ie, i-e and igh

There are different ways to spell the long *i* sound.

ie	i-e	igh
p**ie**	**five**	n**ight**

Activity 1

Can you sort these words into **ie**, **i-e** or **igh** spelling?

high   ride   cried   hike   right   lie   sight

tries   tight   side   like   dried

bright   time   fine

Activity 2

Can you spell the words and use the correct long *i* sound to match the pictures?

a)

k _____

b)

l _____

c)

fr _____

d)

r _____

Activity 3

Can you find the correct spelling to match the picture?

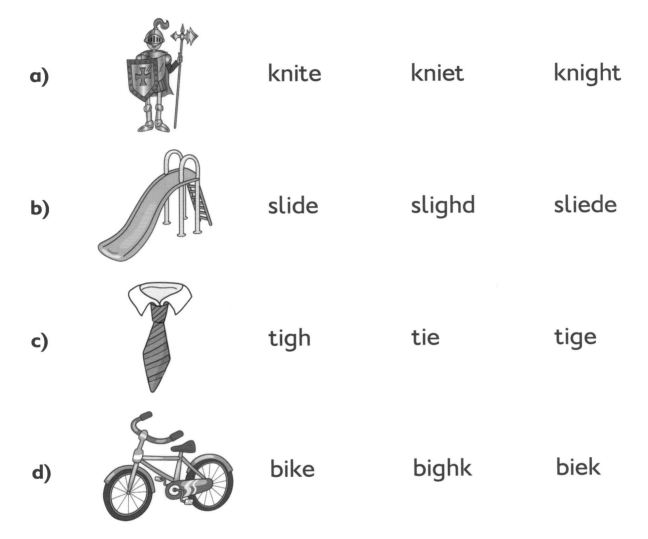

a)   knite   kniet   knight

b)   slide   slighd   sliede

c)   tigh   tie   tige

d)   bike   bighk   biek

Investigate!

Can you list all the different words in the sentences below that have the long *i* sound in?

Last night, at nine o'clock, five of my best friends came to my house to camp out. We tried to make some homemade pie, but we couldn't get it right, so mum bought us ice cream instead! After a lot of playing, we got tired. It was time for bed. We slipped into our sleeping bags and cried, "Goodnight!"

29 ir, ur and er

There are different ways to spell the *er* sound.

ir   ur   er

bir**d**   **f**ur   **wint**er

Activity 1

Can you sort these words into **ir**, **ur** or **er** spellings?

her   term   turn   person   skirt   hurt

under   shirt   church   summer   first

winter   burst   third   sister   squirt

Activity 2

Can you spell the words and use the correct *er* sound to match the pictures?

a)

teach _____

b)

flow _____

c)

b _____ thday

d)

t _____ nip

Activity 3

Can you find the correct spelling to match the picture?

a)   girl   gurl   gerl

b)   skurt   skirt   skert

c)   nerse   nurse   nirse

d)   circle   curcle   cercle

Investigate!

How many *er* words can you find around the classroom?

30 air, ear and are

There are different ways of spelling the *air* sound.

air	ear	are
p**air**	b**ear**	squ**are**

Activity 1

Can you sort these words into **air**, **ear** or **are** spellings?

tear   bare   wear   air   dare   lair   hair

glare   stare   scare   flare

Activity 2

Can you spell the words and use the correct *air* sound to match the pictures?

a)

b)

c)

d)

ch _____   p _____   st _____ s   f _____

Activity 3

Can you find the correct spelling to match the picture?

a) farey   fairy   feary

b) hair   hare   hear

c) cair   care   cear

d) shair   share   shear

Investigate!

Can you list all the different words in the poem with an *air* sound in?

Yesterday we went to the fair
To see the famous big brown bear.
We walked around and found his lair.
His paws were huge and his teeth could scare.
He was happy in the fine fresh air,
Napping in his wooden chair.
All I could do was stand and stare,
The day I saw the big brown bear bare!

31 or, ore, aw and au

There are different ways of spelling the *or* sound.

or	ore	aw	au
f**or**k	sh**ore**	cl**aw**	s**au**ce

Activity 1

Can you sort these words into **or**, **ore**, **aw** or **au** spellings?

more   draw   dinosaur   saw   horse   yawn

wore   short   crawl   for

Activity 2

Can you unscramble the letters to find words to match the pictures?

a)

n or h

b)

k aw h

c)

aw p

d)

n or c

Activity 3

Can you write a sentence about each of these words?

horse   snore   lawn   crawl

Activity 4

Can you use the *or* words below to complete the sentences?

draw   August   yawn

torch   sore

a) In the month of _____ we go on holiday.

b) In the dark you can see with a _____.

c) If I am really tired I _____ a lot.

d) I like to _____ interesting patterns with crayons.

e) My foot is _____ because my red shoe is too small.

Investigate!

How many words can you find around your school which have the *or* sound?

45

32 ph and wh

In some words when you can hear the *f* sound it is spelt as ph.

dolphin   elephant

Activity 1

Can you find the correct spelling to match the picture?

a) trophy   trofy   **b)** telefone   telephone   **c)** photo   foto

In some words when you can hear the *w* sound it is spelt as wh.

wheel   whale

Activity 2

Which is the correct spelling?

a) wistle   whistle   **b)** whisker   wisker   **c)** weat   wheat

33 Compound words

Compound words are two or more words which are joined together.

foot + ball = football

Activity 1

Can you use the words below to make some compound words?

cake   brush   paper   berry

a) news   + _____ = _____

b) pan   + _____ = _____

c) tooth   + _____ = _____

d) straw   + _____ = _____

Activity 2

Can you use the picture clues to help create a new compound word?

a) ⭐ + 🐟 =

b) ✉️ + 📦 =

c) 🌧️ + 🎀 =

34 Common words

There are some common words which do not fit our spelling rules. We need to remember how to spell these words. Some examples are:

the   a   do   today   of   said

says   were   was   is   his

has   your   they   be

Activity 1

Which is the correct spelling of these words?

a)   frend   friend   freend

b)   saum   sume   some

c)   howse   house   howwse

d)   was   wos   woz

e)   skool   scool   school

f)   are   arr   ar

g)   yue   you   yoo

Activity 2

Can you write each of these words in a sentence? Remember that the sentence needs to start with a capital letter and finish with a full stop.

a) today   **b)** they   **c)** push   **d)** are   **e)** once

35 Days of the week

There are seven days in the week. Each day starts with a capital letter for its special name.

Monday

Activity 1

Can you put the seven days of the week in order?

Sunday   Tuesday   Saturday   Monday

Thursday   Wednesday   Friday

Activity 2

Can you answer these questions? Remember to use a capital letter for the day of the week.

a) What day comes after Wednesday?

b) What day comes after Friday?

c) What day comes before Monday?

d) What day comes before Thursday?

e) What day comes after Tuesday?

Investigate!

Can you write down the days of the week and draw a picture about what you do on each day.

49

36 At school

Which of these can you see in your classroom? Make a list and add more!

Activity 2

Which classroom word is being described in each sentence below?

scissors   book   ruler

computer   teacher

a) I live on a shelf and you can read me.

b) You can use me to cut out your picture.

c) I can help you measure how long something is.

d) I help you with your work.

e) You can use me to send messages around the world.

37 Around the home

Activity 1

In which of the rooms below would you find these items? Some of them may be in more than one room.

| bedroom | bathroom | kitchen | living room |

sofa   toothbrush   bath   pan   cooker   vase

rug   curtain   bed   toilet   shower   mirror

radiator   chair

Activity 2

Which word is being described in each sentence below?

bath   carpet   table   oven

lamp   blanket

a) I cover the floor.

b) You heat me up and then cook food in me.

c) You switch me on to give light.

d) I can cover you up and keep you warm.

e) You fill me with warm water and bubbles.

f) You sit at me to eat your dinner.

38 Food

Activity 1

Which of these foods can you see in the picture? Make a list.

chicken   **pumpkin**   **sweet potato**   **corn**

carrots   **tomato**   **onion**   **mushrooms**

avocado   **peas**

Activity 2

Can you sort these foods into vegetables, fruits and meats?

melon   **carrot**   **chicken**   **cucumber**

beans   **pineapple**   **beef**   **peach**

Investigate!

Can you think of a fruit or vegetable that starts with every letter of the alphabet? Work with a friend to create a list.

52

© 2015 Rising Stars UK Ltd.

39 On the farm

Which of these farm words can you see in the picture? Make a list.

tractor **stable** **barn** **pigsty** **pond** **hay**
farmhouse **hen** **scarecrow** **donkey** **bull**

Which farm word is being described in each sentence below?

cockerel **field** **plough**

hens **cow**

a) This is where the sheep go out to eat.

b) This animal wakes everyone up in the morning.

c) These animals give us eggs for our breakfast.

d) This animal makes sure we have milk each day.

e) This tool helps to dig up the soil in the field.

40 Transport

Activity 1

Which of these words do you find in each of these different places? Some of them may be found in more than one place.

| railway station | airport | garage | service station |

pilot **plane** **petrol** **car**

platform **train driver** **bus** **runway**

breakdown truck **helicopter** **train**

Activity 2

Which word or words is being described in each sentence below?

engine **wheels** **car wash** **headlights**

ticket machine

a) These turn to make a car move.

b) You take your car here when it is dirty.

c) At night you switch these on to see.

d) Sometimes you need to put oil in this.

e) You go to this to pay for parking.

Our local area

Activity 1

Which of these words can you see in your local area near school?
Make a list.

shop   pavement   traffic lights   taxi   lamp post
flats   market   street   cafe   van   crossing

Activity 2

Can you fill in the missing letters to describe the pictures?

a)

bicy____le

b)

ho____el

c)

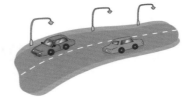

roa____

d)

lorr____

Investigate!

Can you write a sentence for each of the words in Activity 2 above?

42 Feelings

Activity 1

How is the girl feeling in each picture?

a)

s____d

b)

s____ck

c)

an____ry

d)

wor____ied

e)

ha____py

f)

ti____ed

Lever Edge Primary Academy

Investigate!

How many other words can you think of to describe the pictures above?